MIDDLE EASTERN
COOKING

INTERNATIONAL GOURMET

MIDDLE EASTERN
COOKING

Jenny Ridgwell

CRESCENT BOOKS
NEW YORK

Copyright © Ward Lock Limited 1986

First published in Great Britain in 1986 by
Ward Lock Limited, 8 Clifford Street,
London W1X 1RB, an Egmont Company.

This 1987 edition published by Crescent
Books, distributed by Crown Publishers, Inc.,
225 Park Avenue South, New York, New
York 10003.

h g f e d c b a

Printed and bound in Portugal.
ISBN 0-517-62452-4

CONTENTS

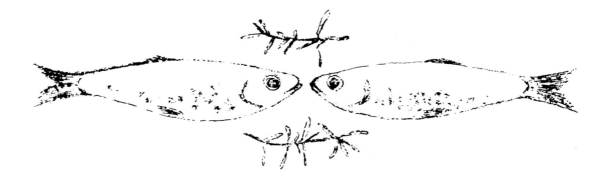

Acknowledgments

Inside photography by James Murphy

Home Economists – Kate Frears and
Tania Leaver

Stylist – Marie O'Hara

Line drawings by Lorraine Harrison

The author would like to thank Berooz
Yazdlani, Sara Godsi, Gila Godsi, Khlas
Kjairallah, Mr. Alandini, Mrs. Shahnaz
Davish, Mrs. Fatima Ahanad Othman for
their recipes and advice.

Note: All recipes serve four people, unless
otherwise specified.

INTRODUCTION

People from the Middle East care deeply about their food. The ingredients must be fresh and of good quality, and much time and effort is spent in food preparation. Their diet is amazingly healthy — they eat plenty of cereals, such as wheat and rice, together with legumes and fresh vegetables. Fruit is usually eaten instead of dessert, although the Middle Eastern sweet tooth gives in to temptation when presented with the delicious traditional rich cakes, and pastries soaked in sugar syrup.

To know a people and their ways, customs, and eating habits is one thing. It is, however, also important to know a little about their geography. The Middle East is made up of the region of South West Asia and North East Africa stretching from Turkey, through Iran, Iraq and Saudi Arabia to the Sudan and the countries bordering the Eastern Mediterranean. Much of the Middle East is desert with only about ten per cent of the land available for cultivation. Because of the shortage of pastureland, few cattle are reared, and sheep, goats and chickens are the main source of meat. Milk from goats and sheep is used to make yogurt and cheese.

Chick peas (garbanzo beans) and lentils have been grown for thousands of years in the Middle East and are an important part of the diet. Other indigenous plants include figs, dates, melons, pomegranates, carrots, cabbage and cauliflower. Wheat came to the Middle East thousands of years ago, and is made into breads and eaten every day, or is used as *burghul* (bulgur) for salads or for thickening soups and stews. Rice arrived later, but is now an important food for Middle Eastern people, and is treated with reverential care.

In the fifth century B.C., Iraq was considered to be one of the wealthiest countries in the world, at the center of the spice-trading route. Today, curry powder is included in quite a number of Iraqi dishes originally introduced by people from the Indian subcontinent who came seeking work. Throughout the Middle Ages, the Arabs controlled the spice trade between East and West, and, as a result, spices such as cinnamon, nutmeg, allspice and saffron, play an important part in Middle Eastern cooking.

Israel is home to people of so many nationalities that it is not surprising to find dishes there from all over the world. Its agriculture is expanding with the introduction and development of new fruits and vegetables. *Felafel*, a type of chick pea rissole, is the national dish, served in pita bread with tahini sauce.

Iran has the most unusual cuisine of the Middle East. Sweet and non-dessert ingredients are often cooked together, such as prunes with lamb or oranges with chicken, and the food is flavored with fresh herbs and spices. A particular speciality is a selection of thick omelets called *kookoos*. *Kookoo Sabzi*, a dark green omelet, is most popular (for recipe, see page 42).

recipe, see page 42).

Yogurt, eaten as a nourishing food, is popular throughout the Middle East, and especially in Iran. It is served in hot and cold soups, with main courses, as a salad and as an iced drink.

Syria, Jordan and Lebanon all enjoy similar tastes in food, especially the famous *mezze*, a selection of delicious dips, salads and snacks. Lebanon, with its strong French influence in the past, has the most sophisticated ways of preparing food.

The recipes for *Middle Eastern Cooking* are from nationals who now live abroad and have learned to adapt locally available foods to their own unique way of cooking. Sometimes the explanation of techniques may seem lengthy, but Middle Eastern attention to detail is important to achieve the authentic finished dish.

Nevertheless, whatever part of the Middle East you draw upon to add to your culinary skills, the results will be excitingly unusual and satisfyingly adventurous for you, your family and your guests.

Ingredients

Most ingredients used in the recipes are readily available, but some are unfamiliar or used in an unfamiliar way, and need special mention.

BREADS
There are many types of Middle Eastern bread, leavened and unleavened, varying in size from thick loaves to thin, flat breads like

Mankoush (see page 32). Bread can be cooked over open fires or baked in ovens. Pita (see page 31) is a flat, soft, hollow bread which may be oval or round in shape and is often filled with salad, cheese or meats and used for snacks. Bread is eaten every day in the Middle East and is often used as a scoop to pick up food.

BURGHUL (Bulgur)

To make *burghul*, whole wheat grains are partially cooked, then dried and cracked. There are three grades – medium and large, frequently used for pilafs and stuffings, and fine *burghul* which is generally used for *kibbehs* and salads. Fine *burghul* should be rinsed before use. The other grades need to be soaked.

HERBS AND SPICES

Fresh parsley, mint, cilantro and dill are frequently used in soups, stuffings, stews and salads. Dried mint fried in a little oil is used for garnish. When fresh herbs are not available, substitute a smaller quantity of dried herbs.

Saffron, the world's most expensive spice, is used to flavor and color rice dishes, stews and some desserts. Pound the stamens to a powder and soak in hot water for at least an hour before use. Turmeric can be substituted, but must be used sparingly since it has a bitter flavor.

Sumac, a red spice with a sour lemony flavor, is made from the dried ground berries of the sumac tree. It is generally used to give color and sharpness to soups, rice and meat dishes and in Iran it is used as a condiment with kebabs and rice. There is no real substitute.

Cardamom has a delicate, slightly lemony flavor. Whole cardamom pods can be split and used in cooking or the seeds can be crushed.

NUTS

Chopped nuts are used as fillings and toppings for cakes and pastries. Whole nuts may be fried and used to decorate rice and non-dessert dishes. Pine nuts, pistachios, walnuts, hazelnuts and almonds are all used in cooking. Remove the brown husk on almonds by soaking the nuts for a few minutes in hot water. The almonds should then pop out of their skins. Leave the nuts to soak in water for a while to plump them up.

Keep a jar of fried nuts in the refrigerator for decorating non-dessert dishes. Heat some butter or oil and lightly fry almonds or pine nuts until golden. Cool and store in a jar. Before use, wrap the nuts in foil and heat in the oven.

Salted pistachios are sold as "nibbles." Use unsalted pistachios for cooking.

PHYLLO AND KUNAFEH PASTRIES
Phyllo (also spelled *filo*) is a thin transparent pastry. It is used to make *Baklava* (see page 90). When baked it becomes crisp, flaky and golden.

Kunafeh is a pastry made only from flour and water and looks like white shredded wheat. It is usually tossed in butter before baking.

Both pastries can be bought from Middle Eastern or Greek delicatessens.

POMEGRANATE JUICE OR SYRUP
This concentrated dark brown juice, made from pomegranates, is used to make dishes such as *Fesenjan* (see page 61) as well as for fruit salads and drinks. It is expensive but well worth trying for its unusual flavor. You can find it in well-stocked Middle Eastern shops.

LEGUMES
Dried legumes, with the exception of brown, green and red lentils, need soaking for at least 5 hours or overnight, the water then being discarded. A little baking soda added to the soaking water will speed up cooking time. Always boil beans rapidly in *fresh* water for at least 10 minutes, before reducing the heat and then cooking until soft. Cooking times will vary according to the age and quality of the beans. A pressure cooker will reduce cooking time. Do not add salt until the end of the cooking time to prevent the beans becoming tough.

Canned beans may be substituted in some recipes to save time. Add towards the end of cooking time since the beans are precooked.

RICE
Rice may be served plain, steamed with meat and vegetables, cooked with herbs, decorated with fried nuts and golden raisins or used for stuffing vegetables.

A selection of ingredients for Middle Eastern cooking

For light, fluffy whole grains, use good quality long-grain rice such as Basmati or Patna. Rinse the rice before cooking to remove excess starch. Iranians like to soak their rice overnight before using it.

Short-grain rice can be used for stuffings since this helps the ingredients to stick together.

ROSE WATER AND ORANGE BLOSSOM WATER
Rose water is distilled from rose petals, and orange blossom water is made from the blossoms of the bitter orange tree. Both can be bought from Middle Eastern and Greek shops as well as drug stores. These blossom waters are used to flavor milk puddings, rice, pastries, and made into syrups and drinks. A recipe for *Atter*, blossom syrup, is on page 92.

TAHINI OR TAHINA
Tahini is a beige-colored paste made from ground sesame seeds and it is used to flavor dips and sauces. It is sold in jars and should be stirred before use as the oil separates from the paste.

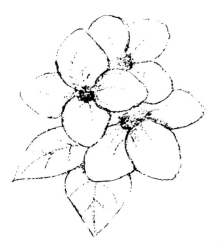

SOUPS

As in most parts of the world, soups, both hot and cold, are an important and well-loved part of Middle Eastern meals. Some of the soups are so nourishing and satisfying that they are a meal in themselves and can be used as a main course, rather than an appetizer.

In Iran, delicious soups are made from sweet as well as savory ingredients — dried fruit combined with meat, for example — and yogurt is often stirred into the soup at the last minute.

The basis for many Middle Eastern soups is a chicken, meat or fish stock, but you may, if you prefer, use a good-quality bouillon cube instead.

Some of the recipes included in this section will be exciting and exotic to some Western tastes, but for everybody who is adventurous enough to risk the unknown, they will soon become firm family favorites.

IRAQ, IRAN
Beet Soup

This soup is similar to Russian bortsch, but without the sour cream, and may be served hot or cold.

3 beets, grated
2½ cups water
1 clove garlic, crushed
juice of 1 lemon

2 teaspoons sugar
salt, freshly ground black pepper
chopped parsley

Place all the ingredients in a saucepan. Boil, cover and simmer for 30 minutes until the beets are cooked. Serve garnished with parsley.

Soup Mast Va Khiar
Cold Yogurt Soup

An unusual sweet and savory cold soup, delicious on hot days.

⅓ cup raisins
⅔ cup water
2 cups plain yogurt
⅔ cup milk
1 cucumber, diced
1 hard-boiled egg, finely chopped

4 scallions, cut into fine rings
salt, freshly ground black pepper
GARNISH:
1 tablespoon chopped fresh or dried dill or 1
* tablespoon fresh chopped parsley*

Soak the raisins in the water for 5 minutes. Drain and discard the water.
  Mix together the yogurt, milk, cucumber, egg and scallions, and season to taste. Stir in the raisins, then add a little water if the soup is too thick. Chill the soup for 1 hour before serving. Serve garnished with dill or parsley.

IRAN

Ashe Mast
Hot Yogurt Soup

This thick soup, flavored with yogurt, is a filling meal on its own.

½ lb. ground beef
1 medium onion, minced
3 leeks, minced
1 lb. fresh spinach very finely chopped or
* 8 oz. frozen chopped spinach*
7 tablespoons short-grain rice
½ cup fresh chopped parsley

1 teaspoon salt
freshly ground black pepper
2½ cups water
1¼ cups plain yogurt
GARNISH:
fried onion rings plus oil from frying

In a large saucepan fry the ground beef in its own fat for 10–12 minutes until the meat begins to brown. Stir in the onion and leeks, and cook for an additional 5 minutes. Add the remaining ingredients except the yogurt, then bring the liquid to a boil, cover and simmer for 20 minutes.
  Stir the yogurt thoroughly into the soup, and serve hot, garnished with fried onion rings and a little oil.

Cold Yogurt Soup

SAUDI ARABIA
Shikamba
Creamy Lamb Soup with Meat Balls

½ lb. stewing lamb, cut into cubes
1 quart water
salt, white pepper
½ cup flour

1 egg yolk
¼ lb. ground lamb
oil
2 tablespoons tomato paste

Boil the lamb in 1 quart salted water until tender. Remove the meat and when cool enough to handle, pull it into shreds.

Mix together the flour, egg yolk, pepper and enough water to form a thin paste. Whisk this paste into the boiling stock, and stir until the soup thickens. Return the lamb, season to taste, cover and cook for 20 minutes.

Mix the ground lamb with a little salt and pepper. Form into grape-sized balls, and shallow-fry in oil until golden-brown. Drain.

Before serving, add the meat balls to the soup. Mix together 2 tablespoons each oil and tomato paste, and pour this in a swirl over the soup.

EGYPT
Shorbet Ads
Lentil Soup

1⅛ cups red or yellow split lentils
2 onions, minced
1 tomato, skinned and chopped
1 carrot, chopped
1 quart water

salt, freshly ground black pepper
2 tablespoons oil
juice of ½ lemon
chopped parsley

Place the lentils, one minced onion, the tomato and carrot in a large saucepan and pour in the water. Boil briskly for 10 minutes, then cook for an additional 20–30 minutes until the lentils are soft. Strain the mixture or purée in a processor to make a smooth soup. Season to taste.

Heat the oil in a skillet and fry the remaining onion until pale brown.

Reheat the soup and add the fried onion and lemon juice. Garnish with chopped parsley, and serve with hot pita bread (page 31).

IRAN
Abgushte Miveh
Dried Fruit Soup

Serves 4–6

---

1 lb. lean stewing lamb or beef, cut into cubes
½ cup yellow split peas
1 medium onion, minced
1 quart water
salt, freshly ground black pepper
½ cup prunes, soaked overnight

½ cup dried apricots, soaked overnight
3–4 whole cloves
1 teaspoon turmeric
½ teaspoon ground cinnamon
juice of 1 lemon (approx.)

Place the meat, split peas and onion in a saucepan, add the water and seasoning. Bring to a boil, then simmer for about 1 hour until the meat is tender. Skim the surface. Add the remaining ingredients, and cook for an additional 20 minutes. Before serving, adjust the seasoning and add more lemon juice if the soup is too sweet.

ISRAEL
Avocado Soup

Serves 4–6

---

2 vegetable bouillon cubes
3 ripe avocados, skinned and pitted
juice of ½ lemon
1¼ cups light cream
chili sauce

salt, freshly ground black pepper
GARNISH:
1 avocado, cubed and tossed in lemon juice

Dissolve the bouillon cubes in a little boiling water and, with cold water, make up to 2½ cups.

Process the avocados in a blender with the lemon juice or mash to make a smooth purée. Blend all the other ingredients together, adding chili sauce to taste. Chill before serving garnished with cubes of avocado.

Variation

Heat the soup very gently in a saucepan until hot enough to serve — it may lose its delicate green color if heated for too long and too fiercely. Serve with cubes of avocado.

MEZZE & APPETIZERS

The delicious eye-catching dips, salads and small snack dishes that make up the *mezze* table are as exciting and interesting as their names. The *mezze* table is a very important and special part of the Middle Eastern way of eating. Middle Eastern meals begin with a mouthwatering array of dips, salads, *kibbeh*, *felafel*, pickles, and olives. All these are served with bread and the food is eaten slowly and leisurely, using fingers and bread to dip into the delicious array of different dishes. While eating, the meal is delightfully punctuated with a glass or two of *arak*, an anise-flavored alcoholic beverage.

A *mezze* table can consist of a small selection of easily prepared, time-saving foods, such as nuts, pickles and feta cheese, or, for special occasions, a large variety of dips. Many of the favorite *mezze* dishes can also be used as appetizers for a three-course meal.

In the Middle East, a great variety of vegetables are pickled and served as part of the *mezze* table or as an accompaniment to main courses. Most of the pickle recipes in this book are ready to use within two weeks of pickling, some sooner, and most will keep for up to two months.

You will very quickly come to appreciate why the *mezze* table is such an appetizing and special part of Middle Eastern mealtimes.

Tabbouleh (page 20)

Tabbouleh
Bulgur and Herb Salad

Serves 4–6

⅔ cup fine bulgur
1 bunch fresh parsley, chopped
2 tablespoons fresh chopped mint or 1
tablespoon dried mint
2 tomatoes, finely chopped
1 bunch scallions, minced

½ onion, grated
1 green pepper, seeded and finely chopped
½ head romaine lettuce
DRESSING:
4 tablespoons olive oil
juice of 2–3 lemons
salt, freshly ground black pepper

Place the bulgur in a strainer and wash with cold water. Squeeze out excess water.

Mix together the dressing ingredients.

Place all the salad ingredients, apart from the romaine, in a bowl, and toss well. Stir in the dressing.

Arrange the romaine leaves on a serving dish and pile on the *tabbouleh*. The traditional way to eat the salad is to scoop it up with the romaine leaves.

EGYPT
Ful Medames
Brown Egyptian Beans with Dressing

Serves 4–6

---

1 lb. brown Egyptian beans or *any small
reddish-brown beans, soaked overnight*
2 cloves garlic, crushed
DRESSING:
4 tablespoons olive oil

4 tablespoons lemon juice
salt, freshly ground black pepper
GARNISH:
4 hard-boiled eggs, quartered
chopped parsley

Discard the soaking water, and cover the beans with fresh water. Bring to a boil and boil briskly for at least 10 minutes, then simmer for 1½–2 hours until the beans are cooked but not too soft. Drain, then mix in the crushed garlic. Mix the dressing ingredients, and pour over the beans.

Serve the beans topped with eggs quartered and sprinkled with parsley.

Cold Stuffed Grape Leaves

Serves 4–6

No meat is used for this stuffing. It is well worth trying fresh grape leaves when in season as the flavor is quite superior to preserved leaves.

½ lb. preserved or fresh grape leaves
juice of 1 lemon
STUFFING:
¼ cup short-grain rice, rinsed several times
1 medium onion, grated
2 tablespoons minced parsley

2 tomatoes, finely chopped
1 teaspoon dried mint
½ teaspoon allspice
½ teaspoon ground cinnamon
1 clove garlic, minced

Prepare the grape leaves according to the package instructions or blanch fresh leaves in boiling water to soften them.

Mix together all the stuffing ingredients. Place 1 teaspoon of stuffing in the center of each leaf. Fold the sides into the middle, then roll up the leaf.

Line the base of a large saucepan with damaged leaves to prevent the rest from sticking. Pack the grape leaves tightly in the pan with the seam underneath. Pour in enough water to cover the grape leaves, add the lemon juice, and cover with a small plate. Bring to a boil, then simmer, covered, for 45 minutes–1 hour until most of the water has been absorbed and the rice is tender.

Serve cold as part of the *mezze* table or as an appetizer.

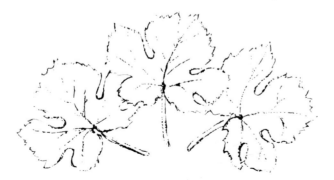

Stuffed Kibbeh
Serves 6–8

This recipe, one of the specialities of the *mezze* table, is served with bread, pickles and other dishes.

KIBBEH:
1 cup fine bulgur
1 lb. good quality ground lamb or *beef*
1 medium onion, grated
1 teaspoon salt
freshly ground black pepper
½ teaspoon ground cinnamon
½ teaspoon ground allspice
oil for baking or *deep-frying*

FILLING:
½ onion, grated
1 tablespoon oil
¼ lb. good quality ground lamb or *beef*
¼ cup pine nuts
freshly ground black pepper
pinch of ground allspice

Rinse the bulgur well, then mix together with the remaining kibbeh ingredients, and either pound to a smooth paste in a mortar and pestle or blend in a food processor. Knead, adding a little ice water so that the mixture becomes very smooth and cool. Chill before use.

To prepare the filling, fry the onion in the oil until soft, then mix together with the other ingredients.

With wet hands divide the kibbeh mixture into 15–20 pieces. Shape each into an oval ball, and make a hole in the middle with your finger. Fill with a little of the filling. Squeeze the mixture closed, then work back into the oval shape. Either deep-fry in hot oil until golden or place on a greased baking sheet, brush with oil and bake for 30–40 minutes in a moderate oven (350°F) until brown.

Serve hot as part of the *mezze* table.

Stuffed Kibbeh with *White Turnip and Beet Relish* and *Mixed Vegetable Relish (page 33)*

Kibbeh Bi Sayniyyi
Baked Stuffed Kibbeh

Serves 4–6

This is one of the easiest *kibbeh* to make – it consists of layers of a meat mixture, baked in the oven.

KIBBEH:
¼ cup fine bulgur
¼ lb. finely ground lamb or beef
1 large onion, finely grated
1 teaspoon ground allspice
salt, freshly ground black pepper
a little oil for glazing

FILLING:
1 medium onion, grated
5 oz. ground lamb or beef
½ teaspoon ground cinnamon
½ cup walnuts, chopped
½ cup raisins, chopped

Prepare the *kibbeh* first. Rinse the bulgur well.

Pound the meat in a mortar and pestle or blend in a food processor to make a smooth paste. Work in the bulgur, onion, allspice and seasoning. Chill.

To prepare the filling, fry the onion and meat together until the meat browns. Add the cinnamon, nuts and raisins.

Spread half the *kibbeh* over a baking sheet. Cover with the filling, and top with the remaining *kibbeh*, smoothing the top with a knife. Score into diamond shapes, and brush with a little oil. Bake in a hot oven (400°F) for 35–40 minutes until browned. Leave to cool slightly before cutting into pieces.

Serve hot or cold as part of the *mezze* or with salad and yogurt.

Kibbeh Nayyi
Raw Kibbeh

Serves 4–6

Use good quality meat, and since the meat is eaten raw, consume on the same day as purchase. Serve as part of the *mezze* or as an appetizer.

⅔ cup medium bulgur
1 lb. lean lamb, finely ground
1 small onion, grated
½ sweet red pepper, grated
½ teaspoon ground cinnamon

salt, freshly ground black pepper
lettuce leaves
olive oil
minced scallions
mint leaves

Soak the bulgur in cold water for 30 minutes, then drain and squeeze out excess water.

Pound the meat in a mortar and pestle or blend in a food processor to form a smooth paste. Work in the bulgur, adding a little ice water to keep the mixture cool. Add the onion, pepper and cinnamon, and season well.

Using wet hands, mold the mixture into oval or round serving-size portions. Chill before serving.

Serve with lettuce leaves, a little oil poured in the center of each portion, and garnish with scallions and mint.

SYRIA

Muhamara
Chopped Nuts with Hot Pepper Sauce

1½ cups mixed finely chopped nuts – walnuts,
pistachios, pine nuts and almonds (not
peanuts)
2 red chili peppers, minced
juice of ½ lemon

chili or Tabasco sauce
salt
olive oil
chopped parsley

Mix together the nuts, chili peppers, lemon juice, chili sauce and salt to taste. Blend in a little olive oil to soften the mixture. Serve in a bowl, and sprinkle with chopped parsley.

Felafel

Serves 4–6

Felafel are popular throughout the Middle East, each country having a slightly different recipe using different beans.

1 lb. chick peas, soaked overnight
3 cloves garlic, crushed
½ teaspoon baking powder
2 teaspoons ground coriander
2 teaspoons ground cumin
1 bunch fresh parsley, minced

1 medium onion, grated
4 scallions, minced
2 tablespoons fresh chopped cilantro
oil for deep-frying

Drain the chick peas. To make the chick peas easier to grind, remove the skins by rubbing with a dish towel. Grind the chick peas in a food grinder or processor, then add the remaining ingredients and work to a smooth paste. Leave to rest for 30 minutes.

With wet hands, shape a spoonful of the mixture into a round patty, 1½ inches in diameter.

Heat the oil and deep-fry the *felafel* until golden-brown. Drain on paper towels.

Serve hot as part of the *mezze* table or place inside pita bread (page 31) with some lettuce, a squeeze of lemon juice and some Tahini Sauce.

Tahini Sauce

Tahini sauce may be served as a salad dressing, as a sauce for *felafel* or as a dip.

⅔ cup tahini (sesame paste)
3–4 tablespoons water
juice of 2 lemons
salt, freshly ground black pepper

2 cloves garlic, crushed
1 tablespoon fresh chopped parsley

Mix the tahini to a smooth paste with the water, then blend in the lemon juice and other ingredients.

Felafel in *Pita Bread (page 31) with Tahini Sauce*

Mast va Khiar
Yogurt and Cucumber

In Iran, yogurt and cucumber may be served as an appetizer or as a salad with rice and kebabs.

1 large cucumber, pared and finely diced
1½ cups plain yogurt
salt, freshly ground black pepper

1 tablespoon fresh chopped dill or 2 teaspoons dried dill

Mix together the cucumber, yogurt, salt and pepper and dill. Chill for 30 minutes before serving.

Baba Ghanoush
Eggplant and Tahini Purée

This dish is said to have been the invention of an Arab lady belonging to the royal harem. The sultan was so pleased that he gave the recipe her name!

1 large eggplant
1 clove of garlic, crushed
juice of 2 lemons
1 tablespoon tahini (sesame paste)
salt

GARNISH:
chopped parsley
cayenne pepper
olive oil

Broil or bake the eggplant in a moderate oven (350°F) until soft, turning once while cooking. While the eggplant is still hot, hold the stalk and strip off the skin, then remove the stalk. If the skin does not pull off easily, just broil lightly and try again. If left to cool with the skin on, the eggplant flesh discolors. Mash the flesh or purée in a food processor. Work in the other ingredients to form a smooth paste, then chill. Serve garnished with parsley and a sprinkling of cayenne pepper, and drizzle on a little olive oil.

Eggplant and Yogurt Dip

This dish may be served as part of the *mezze* or as a dip with pita bread and raw vegetables.

2 medium eggplants
¼ cup olive oil
⅔ cup plain yogurt
1 clove garlic, crushed

salt, freshly ground black pepper
GARNISH:
juice of ½ lemon
paprika
chopped parsley

Broil the eggplants until soft, turning occasionally. Strip off the skin while hot to avoid discoloration of the flesh. Mash the flesh or purée in a food processor. Work in the oil, yogurt, garlic, salt, pepper and lemon juice to make a smooth purée. Serve garnished with a sprinkling of paprika and parsley.

Hummus Bi Tahina
Chick Pea and Tahini Purée

Hummus is one of the most well-known Middle Eastern recipes and is served as part of the *mezze* table and eaten with hot pita bread.

¾ cup chick peas, soaked overnight
2 cloves garlic, crushed
1 teaspoon salt
freshly ground black pepper
6 tablespoons tahini (sesame paste)

juice of 2 lemons
olive oil
paprika
chopped parsley

Discard the soaking water, and cover the chick peas with fresh water. Bring to a boil and boil briskly for at least 10 minutes, then simmer for 1–1½ hours until the chick peas are tender.

Drain and rinse the chick peas. Reserve a few for garnish, then pound the remainder in a mortar and pestle or purée in a food processor to make a smooth paste. Work in the garlic, salt, pepper, tahini and lemon juice, adding a little water if the paste is too thick. Season to taste.

Place the *hummus* in a serving bowl and smooth down. Pour a little oil in the center, and garnish with the reserved chick peas and a sprinkling of paprika and parsley.

Homemade Yogurt

2½ cups whole milk   *1 tablespoon plain yogurt*

Sterilize all the equipment before starting by immersing it in boiling water.
Boil the milk, then let it cool until you can just hold your finger in and count to ten (110°F). Blend some warm milk with the yogurt, then stir in the remaining milk. Pour into a clean bowl, cover with a plate, then wrap it with a warm blanket. Leave undisturbed in a warm place for 6 hours or overnight, until the yogurt has set.

Labne

Labne is a strained yogurt which can be bought from delicatessens and some supermarkets, or you can make your own.

2 cups plain yogurt   *½ teaspoon salt*

Place the yogurt in a cheesecloth bag or in a large square of cheesecloth tied at the corners to form a bag. Hang on a faucet overnight to allow the liquid to drain out, leaving a thicker creamier mixture.
Mix the *labne* with a little salt and serve sprinkled with paprika and olive oil.
Serve as part of the *mezze* table or, Arabian style, for breakfast.

Labne Balls

Balls of strained yogurt can be bought from delicatessens, or made at home from *labne*.

labne   *paprika*

Follow the recipe for *labne* but add a little more salt to the yogurt and leave for 2–3 days to drain. A thicker mixture is formed which can be shaped into small balls, ¾ inch in diameter. These may be stored in a jar of olive oil and kept in the refrigerator.
Serve with a sprinkling of paprika and some hot bread.

Avocado Dip with Tahini
Serves 2–4

This dip may be served with crunchy raw vegetables and pita bread. If diluted with water, it makes an interesting salad dressing.

1 large ripe avocado, skinned and pitted
2 tablespoons tahini (sesame paste)
juice of ½ lemon
salt, freshly ground black pepper
2 tablespoons water

1 tablespoon fresh chopped parsley
GARNISH:
black olives
paprika

Mash the avocado flesh to a smooth paste. Blend in the tahini, lemon juice, salt and pepper, then stir in the water and chopped parsley. Serve garnished with black olives and a sprinkling of paprika.

Pita Bread

1 package compressed yeast or 1 package
*   active dry yeast*
1 teaspoon sugar
⅔ cup warm water

2 cups white bread flour
1 teaspoon salt

Mix the yeast with the sugar and warm water in a cup and set aside in a warm place until the mixture bubbles up, 5-10 minutes.

Sift the flour and the salt into a bowl and stir in enough of the yeast liquid to form a dough. Knead for about 10 minutes until the dough is smooth and elastic. Place in a bowl, cover with greased plastic wrap and leave in a warm place to rise for 1–1½ hours until doubled in size.

Knead the dough lightly, then pull off small balls of dough, and roll out each one into an oval shape, ¼ inch thick.

Place the dough on greased baking sheets, cover with greased plastic wrap or a dish towel and leave in a warm place to rise for 15–20 minutes. Sprinkle with water. Bake in a very hot oven (475°F) for about 10 minutes until firm but not golden. Cool on a wire rack.

Mankoush

A delicious spicy, herbed flat bread, which is quite easy to make and may be served with *mezze* or salads or eaten as a snack.

1 package compressed yeast or *1 package*
  active dry yeast
1 teaspoon sugar
⅔ cup warm water
2 cups white bread flour
1 teaspoon salt

TOPPING:
2 tablespoons dried thyme
1 teaspoon salt
2 tablespoons sumac
(see reference on page 9)
1 tablespoon sesame seeds
¼ cup vegetable oil

Mix the yeast with the sugar and warm water in a cup and set aside in a warm place until the mixture bubbles up, 5-10 minutes.

Sift the flour and salt into a bowl and stir in enough of the yeast liquid to form a dough. Knead for 10 minutes until the dough is smooth and elastic. Place in a bowl, cover with greased plastic wrap, and leave in a warm place to rise for 1–1½ hours, until doubled in size.

Knead the dough lightly, then pull off small balls of dough and roll out each one into a circle, ¼ inch thick.

Place on a greased baking sheet and press each one firmly with the fingertips to make dents all over. The "dents" prevent the dough from puffing up during cooking.

Mix together the topping ingredients, and spoon a little over each circle of dough. Leave to rise for about 10 minutes in a warm place. Bake in a very hot oven, (475°F) for 8–10 minutes until a light gold and firm. Serve hot.

White Turnip and Beet Relish

The beet in this relish gives a red tinge to the white turnip.

1 lb. white turnips, quartered
1 small raw beet, thinly sliced
1¼ cups warm water
⅔ cups white vinegar

2 teaspoons salt
1 tablespoon sugar

Put the turnip into a large glass jar, and arrange the slices of beet on top.

Mix together the water, vinegar, salt and sugar and stir until the sugar is dissolved and the liquid is clear. Fill the jar to the top with the liquid. Cover with a lid, and leave to mature for 1 week before serving.

Note: In the Middle East the relish would be left in the sunlight to mature. Additionally, only the turnip is eaten, the beet being left in the pickle jar or discarded.

Mixed Vegetable Relish

A variety of vegetables may be used for this relish, according to availability.

2 carrots, chopped
cauliflower florets, chopped
2 celery stalks, cut into chunks
2 small red chili peppers, chopped
small whole cucumbers or strips of unpared
  cucumber, chopped

1¼ cups warm water
1¼ cups white vinegar
2 tablespoons coarse sea salt
1 teaspoon sugar

Pack the vegetables into large glass jars.

Mix together the water, vinegar, salt and sugar, and stir until the salt and sugar dissolve. Fill the jars to the top with the liquid using more or less as is necessary. Cover with a lid, and leave to mature for 2 weeks before serving.

Red Pepper Relish

This bright red relish can be made spicier by adding more chili powder.

2 large sweet red peppers, seeded and finely
   sliced
16 oz. canned chopped tomatoes
1 teaspoon chili powder

1 teaspoon salt
1 teaspoon sugar
1 tablespoon white vinegar

Put all the ingredients in a pan and boil the mixture for 15–20 minutes until the mixture has reduced and thickened.

Spoon the mixture into a jar and cover with a lid. This relish will keep in the refrigerator for up to 1 month.

ISRAEL
Eggplant Relish

2 medium eggplants
⅔ cup oil (approx.)
2 green chili peppers, seeded and cut into
   strips
2 cloves garlic, minced

salt, freshly ground black pepper
2 teaspoons cumin seeds
1¼ cups white vinegar
1 scant cup water

Cut the unpared eggplant into strips about ½ inch thick. Heat some of the oil in a large skillet and fry the eggplant until soft. Add more oil if necessary. Drain and leave to cool.

Arrange the eggplant in a large container, and scatter over the chili peppers, garlic, salt, pepper and cumin seeds.

Mix together the vinegar and water, and pour this over the eggplant.

Leave the mixture in the refrigerator for 2 days before serving.

ISRAEL
Avocado Relish

This is an unusual hot, spicy relish made from pieces of unpared avocado. If available, small pitless cocktail avocados could be used.

2 unpared avocados, roughly cut into pieces
1¼ cups water
2 tablespoons coarse sea salt
2 tablespoons white vinegar

4 red or green chili peppers, finely chopped
2 cloves garlic, minced
1-inch piece of peeled ginger root, minced

Place the avocado pieces in a clean glass jar.

Boil together the water, salt and vinegar, then stir in the other ingredients. Pour over the avocados, then cover the jar and leave for 7 days in the refrigerator before serving. Use within 3 weeks.

ISRAEL
Carrot Relish

1 lb. carrots, cut into strips
2½ cups white vinegar
2 tablespoons olive oil

1 tablespoon salt
2 cloves garlic, minced
1 teaspoon ground cumin

Cook the strips of carrot in a little boiling water for 5–7 minutes until just tender. Drain, then place in a clean jar.

Boil together the vinegar, oil, salt, garlic and cumin, and pour this over the carrots. Cover with a lid, and leave for 2 days before serving.

Use within 1 month.

FISH

A generous variety of fish are caught in the seas surrounding the Middle East, and this is reflected in the exciting number of fish dishes which are available in that part of the world. Fresh and tasty as they are, the fish are often simply grilled over charcoal and flavored with lemon juice, olive oil and perhaps a little garlic, or baked whole, stuffed with a variety of fresh herbs.

Two of the most popular sauces to accompany fish are Tahini sauce (see page 26) made from crushed sesame seeds and plenty of parsley, and Tarator Sauce (see page 37) made from ground walnuts. *Kibbeh samak*, the Lenten version of *Kibbeh* (see page 40), is made from pounded fish and bulgur instead of ground meat.

When a particular type of fish is not available, a suitable alternative has been suggested in the recipes.

Grilled Fish with Tarator Sauce

1 whole (2–3 lb.) red mullet, whiting or trout,
   scaled and cleaned
salt
juice of ½ lemon

a little olive oil
chopped parsley
Tarator sauce (page 37)

Make three slashes on each side of the body of the fish. Rub the skin and inside with salt, lemon juice and oil. Broil or bake in a moderate oven (350°F) for about 30–40 minutes. The flesh of the cooked fish will flake easily. Serve hot or cold, garnished with parsley and the Tarator Sauce.

Tarator Sauce
Nut Sauce

2 slices bread, crusts removed
1 cup walnuts, ground
1 clove garlic, crushed

salt, freshly ground black pepper
juice of ½ lemon
olive oil

Soak the bread in water, then squeeze out any excess.

Pound the walnuts with the garlic, salt and pepper in a mortar and pestle, or blend in a food processor. Add the bread, and gradually mix in the lemon juice and enough oil to make a thick, smooth paste.

Serve with broiled or baked fish or chicken.

ISRAEL
Fried Fish with Avocado Sauce

1 cup matzo meal or cracker crumbs
salt, freshly ground black pepper
4 cod steaks
1–2 beaten eggs
oil for frying
AVOCADO SAUCE:
1 tablespoon oil
¼ small onion, grated
1 clove garlic, crushed

1 ripe avocado
1 tablespoon fresh chopped parsley
1 tablespoon lemon juice
salt, freshly ground black pepper
GARNISH:
sprigs of parsley
avocado slices dipped in lemon juice

Season the matzo meal or cracker crumbs with salt and pepper. Dip each cod steak into beaten egg, then coat with the matzo meal or cracker crumbs, shaking off any excess.

Heat the oil and fry the steaks for 3–5 minutes on each side until golden-brown. Drain on paper towels, and keep warm.

To prepare the avocado sauce, heat the oil in a small pan and lightly fry the onion and garlic until soft.

Scoop out the flesh from the avocado, and mash well. Stir into the onion mixture, add the chopped parsley and lemon juice, and season to taste. Heat the sauce, adding a little water if the sauce is too thick.

Serve the sauce hot with the fish, garnished with parsley and slices of avocado.

EGYPT
Fish Kebab

Serves 4–6

1½ lb. haddock, swordfish or monkfish,
cubed
juice of 3 lemons
6 bay leaves

1 teaspoon cumin
salt, freshly ground black pepper
3 tomatoes, quartered

Place the cubes of fish in a bowl. Pour on the lemon juice, bay leaves, cumin, salt and pepper. Cover and chill for 1 hour.

Thread pieces of fish, bay leaf and tomatoes on skewers, and brush with oil. Barbecue or broil until the fish is cooked, turning occasionally.

Serve with rice, salad and Tarator Sauce (page 37).

IRAN
Baked Fish Stuffed with Herbs

Serves 4–6

1½–2 lb. whole trout, grey mullet or whiting
STUFFING:
6 medium onions, sliced
3 tablespoons oil
2 cloves garlic, crushed
½ teaspoon turmeric

½ teaspoon salt
bunch fresh fenugreek, chopped, or bunch of
fresh parsley, chopped and a pinch of
ground fenugreek
juice of 3 lemons
lettuce leaves, shredded
lemon slices

Cut the fish open on the underside from head to tail, leaving the head on. Press out the backbone and remove all bones. Place in an ovenproof dish.

For the stuffing, fry the onions in the oil until golden-brown. Add the garlic, turmeric and salt, and fry for 1–2 minutes. Mix in the fenugreek, or parsley and ground fenugreek, and lemon juice. Cook for 5 minutes.

Push the stuffing inside the fish, reserving a little to cover the top layer of skin. Cover with foil, and bake in a moderately hot oven (375°F) for 20 minutes, then bake uncovered for 10 minutes or until the flesh is cooked.

Carefully remove the layer of stuffing covering the skin. Serve the fish on a bed of shredded lettuce, garnished with lemon slices.

If desired, serve with Tahini Sauce (page 26).

Baked Fish Stuffed with Herbs and Sabzi Polo
(page 73)

Kibbeh Samak
Baked Fish with Bulgur

Serves 4–6

---

1 cup medium bulgur
1 medium onion, finely chopped
1 tablespoon fresh chopped parsley
1 lb. white fish, boned and skinned

grated rind of 1 orange
salt
½ teaspoon white pepper
2 tablespoons oil

Soak the bulgur in cold water for 30 minutes, then drain and squeeze out excess water.

Pound the onion and parsley in a mortar and pestle, or blend in a food processor to form a smooth paste. Add the fish in pieces, and continue mixing. Mix in the bulgur, orange rind, salt and pepper, and knead the mixture together with your hands.

Spread the mixture in a greased ovenproof dish. Cut diagonal lines, through the kibbeh dividing it into diamond shapes. Brush with oil and bake in a hot oven (400°F) for 25–30 minutes until the surface is crisp and lightly golden.

Serve hot or cold with salad.

Samak Bi Tahina
Baked Fish with Tahini Sauce

1 whole (2–3 lb.) trout, whiting or sea bass
   scaled and cleaned
salt, freshly ground black pepper
juice of ½ lemon
a little olive oil
TAHINI SAUCE:
4 tablespoons tahini (sesame paste)
salt, freshly ground black pepper

1 clove garlic, crushed
juice of 1 lemon
4 tablespoons water
2 tablespoons fresh chopped parsley
GARNISH:
chopped lettuce leaves, sliced radish, olives,
   pickles, pine nuts and pomegranate seeds

Cut three slashes on each side of the body of the fish. Rub salt, pepper, lemon juice and olive oil inside the fish and over the skin, and chill for 30 minutes.

Lift the fish on to an ovenproof dish, pour on a little more oil and lemon juice, and cover with foil. Bake in a moderate oven (350°F) for 30 minutes. Remove the foil and cook for an additional 10 minutes until the flesh flakes when tested with a fork. If the fish is to be served cold, remove and leave to cool.

To make the sauce, mix together the tahini, ½ teaspoon salt, pepper to taste and garlic, and gradually stir in the lemon juice, water and parsley.

Serve the fish on a bed of lettuce, decorated with the rest of the garnish. Spoon on some of the tahini sauce, and serve the rest in a separate bowl. Eat hot or cold.

EGG DISHES

The thick omelets made throughout the Middle East and Iran use an adventurous variety of fillings such as vegetables, herbs, meat or chicken. Known as *eggah* in the Middle East generally, and *kookoos* in Iran, the omelets are eaten hot or cold, cut into slices, or cooked and served as part of a *mezze*, or as an appetizer, or as a main course served with salad.

IRAN
Kookoo Sabzi
Fresh Herb Omelet

Serves 3–4

2 tablespoons oil
4 leeks, minced
½ lb. fresh spinach, very finely shredded
2 tablespoons finely chopped fresh parsley
2 tablespoons finely chopped fresh dill or 1
  tablespoon dried dill

2 cloves garlic, crushed
½ teaspoon baking soda
salt, freshly ground pepper
5 large eggs, lightly beaten

Heat the oil in an 8-inch omelet pan and gently fry the leeks, spinach, parsley, dill and garlic, stirring and tossing with a wooden spoon, until the leeks soften. Set aside to cool a little.

Stir the baking soda, leek mixture, salt and pepper into the beaten eggs, then return the mixture to the omelet pan, and cook for about 20 minutes until the underside is well browned and crisp and the mixture is firm. Turn the *kookoo* over and cook for about 5 minutes until the underside is just beginning to brown.

Serve hot or cold, cut into wedges.

Kookoo Sabzi accompanied by *White Turnip*
and Beet Relish (page 33)

EGYPT
Shakshooket Beid
Tomato, Onion and Parsley Omelet

Serves 2

---

3 tablespoons oil
2 onions, cut into rings
4 tomatoes, skinned and sliced
1 tablespoon chopped parsley

salt, freshly ground pepper
4 eggs, lightly beaten

Heat the oil in a skillet, and fry the onion for about 10 minutes until golden, stirring occasionally. Add the tomatoes, parsley, salt and pepper, and simmer for an additional 5 minutes. Pour the eggs over the mixture and leave to cook until the egg mixture has set. Serve hot, with bread.

IRAN
Kookoo Bademjan
Eggplant Soufflé

Serves 2–4

The eggplant gives a delicious delicate flavor to this *kookoo*.

2 medium eggplants
juice of ½ lemon

salt, freshly ground pepper
4 eggs, separated

Broil or bake the eggplant in a moderate oven (350°F) until soft, turning once during cooking. While still hot, strip off the skin. If it does not peel away easily, broil the skin until crisp and try again. Mash the eggplant flesh well, then add the lemon juice, and season well. Stir in the egg yolks.

In a clean bowl, beat the egg whites until just stiff. Fold in a little of the eggplant mixture, then carefully add the rest. Overbeating will flatten the mixture and prevent it from rising.

Pour into a greased 8-inch round cake pan, and bake in a moderately hot oven (375°F) for 45 minutes until well-risen and golden-brown. Serve immediately with yogurt and salad, or eat cold.

MEAT & POULTRY

Lamb is by far the most popular meat in the Middle East, although beef is also widely used. Pork is forbidden by Jewish and Muslim dietary rules, so is not usually available. Many Middle Eastern recipes use ground lamb, probably because in the past this was the way to tenderize tough meat. Chicken is grilled, stuffed with a variety of fruits, vegetables and rice mixtures, cooked with rice or made into tasty stews.

Additionally, vegetables and meats are often cooked together and are usually served as a main-course dish.

IRAN
Chelo Kebab
Lamb Kebabs with Chelo rice

Serves 4–6

1½ lb. lean ground lamb	TO SERVE (per person):
3 onions, grated	Chelo (page 72)
½ teaspoon powdered saffron	egg yolk in shell
salt, freshly ground black pepper	sumac (see reference on page 9)
2 egg yolks	1 whole broiled tomato

Place the meat in a bowl, spread with the onions, cover and leave to marinate in the refrigerator for 2–3 hours. Mix the saffron with a few drops of hot water.

Remove the meat from the refrigerator, and brush off the onion. Mix the meat with salt, pepper, saffron and egg yolks.

Wet your hands and mold the mixture around skewers, forming a long sausage shape, then barbecue or broil, turning frequently, until well browned.

Serve with *Chelo*, egg yolk in a shell, *sumac* and a broiled tomato for each person.

ISRAEL, YEMEN
Shishlik
Lamb and Vegetable Kebabs

Serves 4–6

1½ lb. lean lamb, cut into 1-inch cubes
MARINADE:
2 tablespoons olive oil
juice of 1 lemon
salt, freshly ground black pepper
1 eggplant, cut into chunks and parboiled

4 small onions, cut into quarters
1 green pepper, seeded and cut into chunks
12 cherry tomatoes or 3 medium tomatoes,
  quartered
oil for brushing

Place the meat in a large bowl. Mix together the marinade and pour over the meat. Toss, cover and refrigerate for about 1 hour.

Thread the cubes of meat on a skewer alternating with pieces of eggplant, onion and pepper and threading on one or two pieces of tomato. Brush the *shishlik* with oil, and barbecue or broil until the meat is cooked, turning frequently.

LEBANON
Calf's Liver in Sour Sauce

1 lb. calf's liver, sliced
2 tablespoons oil
1 medium onion, minced
2 tablespoons flour
1 clove garlic, crushed

2 tablespoons wine vinegar
1 tablespoon tomato paste
salt, freshly ground black pepper
⅔ cup water
pinch of dried or fresh chopped mint

Fry the liver in the oil until lightly browned on both sides. Remove from the pan and keep warm.

In the same pan, fry the onion until soft. Stir in the flour, garlic, vinegar and tomato paste. Season well, then gradually add the water, using more if the sauce appears dry. Bring to a boil, then simmer for 5 minutes. Add the liver, cover and cook for 10 minutes. Serve hot, sprinkled with mint.

Shishlik

Khoresh Bademjan
Eggplant and Lamb Stew

Serves 2–4

This dish is often served at festive occasions and is believed to have been a favorite of kings.

2 medium eggplants
1 tablespoon salt
4 tablespoons butter
2 large onions, sliced
1 green pepper, sliced

1 lb. lean stewing lamb or *beef, cut into cubes*
8 oz. canned chopped tomatoes
juice of ½ lemon
salt, freshly ground black pepper
oil for frying

Cut the eggplants lengthwise into 5–6 slices. Place in a colander, sprinkle with salt, cover with a plate and allow to drain for 30 minutes to remove any bitterness.

Melt the butter in a large saucepan, and quickly sauté the onions, pepper slices and meat. Add the tomatoes, lemon juice and seasoning. Cover and simmer for 40 minutes over low heat.

Wash the salt from the eggplant and dry the slices. Heat some oil in a pan, and fry the eggplant slices for 5–7 minutes on each side until lightly browned and soft. Arrange the slices over the meat, and cook, uncovered, for 10–15 minutes until a thick brown sauce begins to form. Cover and cook for an additional 10 minutes or until the meat is tender. Serve hot, with plain or *chelo* rice (page 72).

Roast Persian Lamb
Serves 6–8

The basting of butter, mint and turmeric transforms a leg of lamb into a dish fit for special occasions.

3–4 lb. leg of lamb
6 cloves garlic, cut in half lengthwise
1 stick (4 oz.) butter
2 tablespoons tomato paste
1 tablespoon fresh chopped mint

1 teaspoon turmeric
salt, freshly ground pepper
2 onions, quartered
3 carrots, sliced

Cut twelve slashes in the lamb flesh using a sharp knife, and into each place half a garlic clove. Put the lamb in a roasting pan.

Mix together the butter, tomato paste, mint, turmeric and salt and pepper. Rub this mixture into the lamb. Surround the lamb with the onions and carrots, and cover the pan with foil. Bake for 30 minutes in a very hot oven (450°F). Baste, then reduce the oven temperature to hot (400°F) and bake for another hour. Finally, reduce the oven temperature to moderate (350°F) and cook until the lamb is juicy and tender (see **Note**). Leave the meat uncovered for the last 15 minutes, for the skin to become crisp.

Serve with salad and rice.

Note: Roasting time for lamb – allow 25 minutes for each pound plus an additional 25 minutes at the end.

Arayess
Stuffed Arabic Bread

A snack of Arabic bread, stuffed with spicy minced lamb or beef with parsley.

1 medium onion, finely chopped
1 tablespoon oil
1 lb. good quality ground lamb or beef
1 bunch parsley, minced

salt, freshly ground black pepper
½ teaspoon ground cinnamon
4–6 pita breads

Fry the onion in the oil until it softens, then stir in the meat and cook an additional 8–10 minutes until the meat has browned. Add the parsley, salt, pepper and cinnamon, and cook for 2 minutes. Drain off any excess fat.

Split open the pockets of the bread, and fill with the meat mixture. Bake in a moderately hot oven (375°F) for 10 minutes. Cut in half and serve hot, with salad.

Kofta Meshweya
Broiled Ground Meat Kebabs

Kofta are eaten throughout the Middle East, each country having its own recipe. It is important to use good quality ground lamb or beef.

1 lb. finely ground lamb or beef
1 onion, grated
1 beaten egg
½ teaspoon ground cinnamon

½ teaspoon ground allspice
1 teaspoon salt
freshly ground black pepper
1 tablespoon fresh chopped parsley

Mix together the ingredients in a bowl, then knead with your hands or blend in a food processor to make a very smooth mixture.

Divide the mixture into 10 equal portions. With wet hands, shape the mixture into sausage shapes around 5 greased skewers, allowing 2 portions per skewer. Broil or barbecue, turning once, until the *kofta* are well-browned.

Serve like a sandwich in pita bread or with plain rice and salad.

Broiled Ground Meat Kebabs and *Onion Salad*
with Sumac (page 77)

Spinach and Minced Meat Kofta
Serves 4–6

---

2 lb. fresh spinach or *1 lb. frozen spinach,
defrosted*
a little oil
1 lb. good quality ground lamb or *beef*
KOFTA:
1 clove garlic, crushed
*2 tablespoons fresh chopped cilantro or 1
teaspoon ground cilantro*

1 tablespoon fresh chopped dill or *1 teaspoon
dried dill*
2 tablespoons ground rice or rice flour
1 medium onion, grated
salt, freshly ground black pepper
1 tablespoon tomato paste

Wash and shred the spinach leaves. Place in a large saucepan with a very little water. Boil, then cover and cook for 10 minutes until the spinach is tender. Drain well, reserving the liquid. Leave to cool. At this stage the defrosted frozen spinach can be used. Press the spinach *very* well in a colander to squeeze out excess juice.

Meanwhile, mix together the ingredients for the *kofta*.

Mix the spinach with the *kofta*, take tablespoons of the mixture and mold in your hands to form 2½ inch long oval sausage shapes.

Pour a little oil into a large saucepan, and arrange the *kofta* in layers. Heat gently until the *kofta* give out some juice, then cover and simmer for 30 minutes. Add a little spinach water to the saucepan, if necessary. Serve hot, with rice, bread and salad.

JORDAN
Mansaaf
Lamb with Yogurt

Serves 4–6

Mansaaf is the national dish of Jordan. Traditionally, the Bedouin will kill a whole lamb for a guest at the feast, who is presented with the eyeballs. The lamb is served with rice and bread and eaten the Bedouin way, with the right hand. This recipe is an adaptation.

1½ lb. lean lamb, cubed
1 onion, cut into chunks
1 teaspoon salt
2½ cups water

2 cups plain yogurt
2 tablespoons cornstarch
1 tablespoon oil
½ cup pine nuts or slivered almonds

Boil together the meat, onion, salt and water in a covered saucepan for 45 minutes–1 hour until the lamb is tender. Drain off the meat and reserve the stock.

Blend the yogurt and cornstarch, and heat gently in a saucepan until just bubbling. Add 1¼ cups meat stock together with the lamb. Bring to a boil, then cook for 10 minutes.

Heat the oil in a pan, and fry the nuts until golden.

Serve the meat and yogurt on a bed of rice garnished with the fried nuts.

Laham Bil Ajeen
Middle Eastern Pizza

Serves 4–6

Similar to an Italian pizza, except that the bread-like base is topped with meat and vegetables.

BASE:
1 package compressed yeast or *1 package active dry yeast*
1 teaspoon sugar
⅔ cup warm water
2 cups white bread flour
½ teaspoon salt
TOPPING:
½ lb. ground lamb or *beef*

1 onion, minced
1 green pepper, seeded and finely chopped
8 oz. canned chopped tomatoes, drained
1 clove garlic, crushed
1 tablespoon tomato paste
salt, freshly ground black pepper
½ teaspoon allspice
1 tablespoon fresh chopped parsley

Mix the yeast with the sugar and warm water in a cup and set aside in a warm place until the mixture bubbles up, 5–10 minutes.

Sift the flour and the salt into a bowl and stir in enough of the yeast liquid to make a dough. Knead for about 10 minutes, then place in a bowl, cover with greased plastic wrap and leave in a warm place to rise for about 1 hour until doubled in size.

Mix together the ingredients for the topping.

Divide the dough in half, shape each piece into a ball, and roll out on a floured surface into a circle about ¼ inch thick. Place each pizza on a greased baking sheet, and cover with the topping. Bake in a very hot oven (450°F) for 15–20 minutes until cooked but still soft underneath.

Note: The pizzas are normally eaten rolled up.

Laham Bil Karry
Meat Curry
Serves 5–6

A mild curry from Iraq made slightly sour by the addition of lemon juice and vinegar.

4 tablespoons oil
1½–2 lb. lean stewing lamb or beef, cubed
4 medium onions, finely chopped
2 cloves garlic, crushed
10 cardamom pods, seeds removed and
   crushed
1 tablespoon curry powder or paste

½ teaspoon ground cinnamon
16 oz. canned chopped tomatoes
juice of ½ lemon
1 tablespoon wine vinegar
1¼ cups water
salt, freshly ground black pepper

Heat the oil in a large saucepan and fry the cubes of meat until they begin to brown. Remove the meat from the pan.

Fry the onions and garlic in the same pan for 5–6 minutes until the onion softens. Stir in the cardamom seeds, curry powder or paste, and cinnamon, and fry for 2–3 minutes. Mix in the chopped tomatoes, lemon juice and vinegar. Bring the sauce to a boil, then simmer for 2 minutes.

Return the meat to the pan and add enough water just to cover the meat. Season with salt and pepper, then cover and simmer for 1½–2 hours until the meat is tender. If the sauce evaporates too much during cooking, add more water.

Before serving, skim off any surface fat using a spoon, and adjust the seasoning. Serve hot, with rice and chutneys.

Mihshi Kousa B'Lubban
Stuffed Zucchini with Yogurt Sauce

Serves 4–6

12–14 medium zucchini
chopped parsley
STUFFING:
6 tablespoons short-grain rice
¼ lb. ground lamb or beef
salt, freshly ground black pepper

½ teaspoon ground cinnamon
1 tablespoon fresh chopped parsley
SAUCE:
2 cups plain yogurt
2 tablespoons cornstarch

Wash the zucchini and trim off one end. Scoop out the soft pulp using an apple corer, knife or special long scoop (see **Note**). Take care not to damage the zucchini skin.

Mix together all the stuffing ingredients, and use to half fill each zucchini, allowing space for the rice to swell during cooking.

Arrange the zucchini in a large saucepan. Just cover with salted water. Bring to a boil, then simmer for 40 minutes until the zucchini are tender. Drain and keep warm on a serving dish.

Blend together the yogurt and cornstarch, and heat gently in a saucepan.

Pour the sauce over the zucchini, and serve hot, sprinkled with chopped parsley.

Note: Special scoops to remove the central pulp from zucchini can be bought.

IRAN
Kufteh Tabrizi
Stuffed Meat Balls

These spicy meat balls are filled with hard-boiled egg and prunes and are the size of large tennis balls – a version the size of a soccer ball is stuffed with a whole chicken!

½ cup split yellow lentils
2½ cups water
1 lb. good quality ground beef
1 egg, beaten
1 teaspoon lemon juice

½ teaspoon ground cinnamon
¼ teaspoon grated nutmeg
salt, freshly ground pepper
2 hard-boiled eggs
6 prunes, soaked overnight, then pitted

Cook the lentils in the water for 30–40 minutes until soft. Drain well, then mash to a purée.

Mix together the meat, egg, lemon juice, spices and salt and pepper to taste in a bowl. Use your hands to work in the lentil purée.

Divide the mixture into two equal portions. Shape into large balls, putting 1 egg and 3 prunes in the center of each ball.

Place in a roasting pan half filled with water, and bake for 45–50 minutes in a moderate oven (350°F) until the meat is cooked. Serve hot with *Chelo* (page 72).

IRAQ
Tashreeb Leban
Meat Balls in Yogurt Sauce

Tashreeb recipes are popular in Iraq but are not found often in other Middle Eastern countries. Bread is used in the dishes to soak up delicious sauces made from meat, vegetables and, in this case, yogurt.

1 lb. good quality ground beef
½ teaspoon allspice
salt, freshly ground black pepper
2 tablespoons oil

2 cups plain yogurt
1 clove garlic, crushed
4 slices bread, crusts removed and cut into
*   strips*
chopped fresh or *dried mint*

Work together the meat, allspice, salt and pepper until they are thoroughly mixed. Divide the mixture into small walnut-sized balls. Heat the oil in a skillet and fry the meat balls until crisp and golden-brown. Set aside and keep warm.

Gently warm the yogurt in a saucepan, adding the garlic and salt to taste. Do not overheat the mixture or the yogurt will curdle.

Line a serving dish with strips of bread. Pour on the sauce, and spoon in the meat balls. Serve hot, garnished with mint.

Mihshi Malfouf
Stuffed Cabbage Leaves
Serves 4–6

Recipes for stuffed cabbage leaves are popular in many parts of the Mediterranean including the Arab countries of the fertile crescent, as well as Greece and Turkey.

1 medium whole green cabbage, with firm
  outer leaves
juice of 1 lemon
dried mint
FILLING:
¾ lb. ground beef

1 medium onion, grated
½ teaspoon allspice
½ teaspoon ground cinnamon
pinch of grated nutmeg
½ cup short-grain rice
salt, freshly ground black pepper

Carefully separate the cabbage leaves by cutting out the central core. Dip the leaves in boiling water for 3–4 minutes until they begin to wilt. Drain, cool and cut out the thick end of the stalks. Cut very large leaves in half, if necessary.

Prepare the filling. Fry the beef in its own fat until it browns, then stir in the onion, spices and rice, and season well.

Put 2 teaspoons of filling at the end of each leaf, fold the sides of the leaf into the middle, and roll up from the filling end into a sausage shape. Continue until all the filling is used up.

Line a saucepan with a few unused cabbage leaves to prevent the rolls from sticking. Make layers of the cabbage rolls, tucking the seam underneath and packing them tightly. Cover with salted water, bring to a boil, cover and simmer for 1 hour, adding more water if necessary.

Five minutes before serving, stir in the lemon juice and a sprinkling of dried mint. Serve hot.

Stuffed Peppers and Onions
Serves 4–6

---

2 large onions
1⅛ cups long-grain rice
6 medium green peppers
½ lb. ground beef
1 medium onion, grated

2 cloves garlic, crushed
½ teaspoon turmeric
4 scallions, minced
salt, freshly ground black pepper
sprigs of mint

Skin the onions and cut off the root end. Make a cut down the side of each onion from top to bottom, through to the center.

Fill a large saucepan with boiling water, and cook the rice and onions together for 10 minutes. Drain and remove the rice.

Drain the onions and allow to cool slightly before carefully pushing out the centers, leaving an onion shell. Chop and reserve the centers of the onions.

Cut off the tops of the peppers and remove the seeds. Stand the peppers and their tops in boiling water for 10 minutes to soften the flesh, then drain. For the stuffing, mix together the rice, ground beef, grated onion, garlic, turmeric, scallions and the reserved chopped onions, and season to taste.

Fill each onion shell with some of the stuffing, and, if necessary secure with a wooden toothpick. Fill each pepper with the remaining stuffing, and replace the tops. Stand the vegetables in a roasting pan, and pour in about 5 cups water. Cover with foil and bake in a hot oven, (400°F) for 30–40 minutes.

Serve with rice and relishes.

Fesenjan
Chicken with Walnut and Pomegranate Sauce

Serves 4–6

Fesenjan is a traditional and popular dish often served on festive occasions. The walnuts and pomegranate sauce give it a delicious and unusual sweet and sour taste, quite unlike any other recipe. If pomegranate juice is not available, substitute lemon juice, a little brown sugar and tomato paste.

3 tablespoons oil
4 chicken breasts, skinned
1 onion, minced
2 cups ground walnuts

¼ cup pomegranate juice (see reference on page 10)
1¼ cups water
salt, freshly ground black pepper

Heat the oil in a pan, and fry the chicken breasts for 4–5 minutes on each side until a light golden-brown. Take care that the flesh does not stick to the pan. Remove from the pan and keep warm.

In the same pan, fry the onion until it just begins to brown. Stir in the ground walnuts, and continue cooking for 2–3 minutes before adding the pomegranate juice, water and salt and pepper. Bring to a boil, then cover and simmer for 35–40 minutes until the chicken is cooked. Serve hot with plain rice.

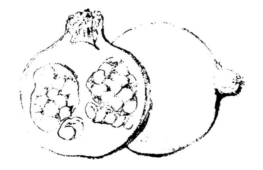

Chicken Stuffed with Rice, Almonds and Golden Raisins

Serves 4–6

3-4 lb. chicken
salt
3 tablespoons tomato paste
⅔ cup water
STUFFING:
½ cup long-grain rice

½ cup slivered almonds
2 tablespoons butter
½ cup golden raisins
juice of ½ lemon
freshly ground black pepper
2 teaspoons sumac *(optional)*

Rub the skin and inside of the chicken with salt.

To make the stuffing, cook the rice for 10 minutes in plenty of boiling water, then drain.

Fry the almonds in the butter for 3–4 minutes until golden.

Mix together the rice, butter and almonds, golden raisins, lemon juice, salt and pepper and *sumac*, if used.

Push the stuffing tightly into the chicken, and secure the opening with two skewers. Place the chicken in an ovenproof dish with any remaining stuffing underneath the bird.

Mix together the tomato paste and water, and pour this over the chicken. Cover the dish with foil or a lid and cook in a hot oven (400°F) for 1–1½ hours until the chicken is cooked. Baste occasionally with the tomato liquid. Uncover the dish for the final 10 minutes to brown the chicken skin. Serve hot.

*Chicken Stuffed with Rice, Almonds and
Golden Raisins*

ISRAEL
Chicken with Pomegranates

¼ cup oil
2 medium onions, sliced into rings
1 clove garlic, crushed
4 chicken breasts, skinned
2 pomegranates
2 tablespoons pomegranate
  juice (page 10) or 2 tablespoons lemon juice

GARNISH:
salt, freshly ground black pepper
½ cup slivered almonds
sprigs of parsley

Heat the oil in a pan, and fry the onion rings and garlic until just beginning to brown. Remove, then carefully fry the chicken breasts for 7–8 minutes on each side. Take care that the flesh does not stick to the pan. Remove the chicken from the pan and keep warm.

Cut the pomegranates in half and scoop out the red seeds. Discard all the yellow pith. Stir the pomegranate seeds and pomegranate juice or lemon juice into the pan. Add the onions and enough water to make a thin sauce. Place the chicken in the sauce, season to taste, cover and simmer for 15 minutes. Serve hot, sprinkled with slivered almonds and garnished with parsley.

ISRAEL
Chicken with Honey and Orange Juice
Serves 4–6

1 3-4 lb. chicken
salt, freshly ground black pepper
2 onions, sliced
¼ cup honey

2 tablespoons oil
⅓ cup orange juice
GARNISH:
orange slices

Rub the skin and inside of the chicken with salt. Place the onions in a roasting pan, and put the chicken on top.

In a saucepan heat the honey, oil and orange juice until the honey dissolves. Season with pepper.

Spoon some sauce inside the chicken, and pour the rest over the top. Bake in a hot oven (400°F) for 1¼–1½ hours, basting from time to time with the juice. Serve garnished with orange slices.

IRAN
Adas Polo
Rice, Green Lentils and Chicken with Golden Raisins

Serves 4–6

A rather unusual dish of rice, colored with green lentils and cooked with a filling of chicken, yogurt and sultanas.

FILLING:
1 medium onion, finely chopped
¼ cup butter
2 boneless chicken breasts, sliced
2 tablespoons oil
½ cup golden raisins
1 teaspoon cinnamon
⅔ cup plain yogurt
½ teaspoon powdered saffron dissolved in
  water

1 tablespoon cornstarch
RICE:
¼ cup green lentils
1 lb. Basmati or long-grain rice, soaked
  overnight
1 teaspoon turmeric
1 teaspoon ground cinnamon
salt, freshly ground black pepper

Make the filling first. Fry the onion in 4 tablespoons of the butter until soft. Remove from the pan and set aside. Fry the sliced chicken breasts in the oil for 5–6 minutes until just beginning to brown. Add the onion, golden raisins and cinnamon. Blend together the yogurt, saffron liquid and cornstarch, and pour into the pan. Bring gently to a boil, then simmer for 15–20 minutes adding a little water if necessary.

Prepare the rice mixture. Boil the lentils in water until tender and drain in a strainer. Drain the rice, and boil in plenty of water for 8 minutes until still chewy, then drain again. Mix in the lentils, turmeric, cinnamon, salt and pepper.

Melt half the remaining butter in a large saucepan with 2 tablespoons water. Spoon in half the rice mixture. Spread on the chicken, and cover with the remaining rice, building into a cone shape. Make three holes with a spoon handle to let out the steam. Dot with the remaining butter. Heat for 5–6 minutes until the rice steams. Cover with a tight-fitting lid, and cook over low heat for 45 minutes–1 hour.

Serve hot, with yogurt and relishes.

Shirin Polo
Chicken with Orange and Saffron Rice

2 chicken breasts
salt, freshly ground black pepper
1⅛ cups long-grain rice, soaked overnight
4 carrots, cut into thin strips
1 stick (4 oz.) butter

¼ cup blanched almonds
⅔ cup candied orange peel, cut into strips (see **Note**)
a pinch of saffron, soaked in 2 tablespoons warm water

Place the chicken breasts in a pan, cover with water, season with salt and pepper, and bring to a boil, then simmer for 15 minutes. Add the rice and more water if necessary, and cook for an additional 10 minutes. Strain the rice and the chicken. Cut the chicken into strips.

Boil the carrots in a little water for 7–10 minutes until just tender. Drain.

Melt half the butter in a pan, and fry the almonds until golden. Stir in the chicken, carrots and ⅓ cup orange peel, and cook for 10 minutes, stirring occasionally.

Melt the rest of the butter with 2 tablespoons water in a large saucepan. Spoon half the rice into the pan, cover with half the chicken mixture, then a little more rice and the remaining chicken. Pile on the rest of the rice, building into a cone shape. Make three holes with a spoon handle to let out the steam. Heat until the steam rises. Cover with a tight-fitting lid, and cook over a low heat for 30 minutes until a crust forms at the bottom. Leave the pan to stand in cold water for 5 minutes to loosen the crust. Just before serving, sprinkle the saffron liquid over the rice, and garnish with the remaining orange peel.

Note: Candied orange peel may be difficult to buy. Make your own by paring the rind off two oranges and leaving it to soak for 2–3 hours. Drain, then boil the rind in fresh water for 5–10 minutes. Drain and stir in 2 tablespoons sugar. Leave the rind to dry on kitchen towels overnight, then cut into strips.

Shirin Polo

VEGETABLES, LEGUMES & SALADS

In the Middle East, the choice of fresh, seasonal, good-quality vegetables is important. Popular vegetables include eggplant, onions, tomatoes, zucchini, peppers and okra. Salads are often finely chopped, mixed with a liberal helping of fresh herbs and tossed in a simple dressing of lemon juice, olive oil, salt and pepper. Tahini or Avocado Sauce (see pages 26 and 37), also make interesting salad dressings. Legumes such as lentils and chick peas are frequently used. Lentils may be substituted for meat when stuffing vegetables.

Okra with Tomatoes and Onions
Serves 4–6

This dish may be served hot or cold, on its own with bread or as a side dish with meat and rice.

1 lb. young, green okra
2 tablespoons oil
2 cloves garlic, chopped
1 medium onion, finely sliced

16 oz. canned chopped tomatoes
salt, freshly ground black pepper
juice of 1 lemon

Wash the okra, wipe off any hairs using a paper towel, and trim off the stems. Take care not to cut into the okra or this will release a sticky fluid during cooking.

Heat the oil in a saucepan and fry the garlic and onion until light gold. Stir in the tomatoes, seasoning, lemon juice and okra. Try to avoid damaging the okra. Add a little water if necessary. Bring to a boil, then cover and simmer for 40–45 minutes until the okra are tender. Serve hot or cold.

Borani Gharch
Mushrooms in Yogurt

Serves 2–4

½ lb. mushrooms, chopped
1 medium onion, finely chopped
4 tablespoons butter

⅔ cup plain yogurt
salt, freshly ground black pepper
chopped parsley

Fry the mushrooms and onions in the butter until they are soft. Drain and cool.

Mix together the mushrooms, onion, yogurt, salt and pepper. Chill for 30 minutes before serving garnished with chopped parsley. Serve as a salad or as an appetizer with bread.

IRAN

Borani Bademjan
Eggplant and Yogurt

---

2 eggplants
salt
oil for frying

2 cloves garlic, slivered
⅔ cup plain yogurt

Cut the eggplants in half lengthwise, then cut across into ½-inch slices. Sprinkle with salt, and leave to stand for 30 minutes to remove bitter juices. Wash and dry the eggplant slices.

Heat the oil in a pan, and fry the eggplant slices until a light gold on both sides. Add the garlic, and fry gently.

Drain the eggplant and garlic on paper towels.

Spread the yogurt on a serving dish, and arrange the eggplant slices and garlic on top.

Koshary
Rice, Macaroni and Lentils with Tomato Topping

Koshary is a vegetarian meal, providing protein from rice, wheat and lentils. It is usually served with salad and relishes.

1⅛ cup brown lentils
1 cup elbow macaroni
½ cup long-grain rice
salt, freshly ground black pepper
SAUCE:
2 onions, minced
2 cloves garlic, crushed

2 tablespoons oil
16 oz. canned chopped tomatoes
1 tablespoon wine vinegar
1 fresh or dried red chili pepper, chopped or
    crumbled
1 tablespoon fresh chopped parsley
salt, freshly ground black pepper

Place the lentils in a saucepan, and cover with plenty of boiling water. Bring to a boil, then cover and simmer for 30–50 minutes, depending upon the age and size of the lentils. Drain the lentils.

Meanwhile, prepare the sauce. Fry the onions and garlic in the oil for 5–10 minutes until the onions soften. Stir in the tomatoes, vinegar and chili pepper, and simmer for 10 minutes or until the mixture thickens. Add the parsley, and season to taste.

While the sauce is cooking, boil the macaroni and rice together in a saucepan of water for 12 minutes. Drain.

Mix together the lentils, macaroni and rice, season to taste, and place on a heated serving dish.

To serve, pour the tomato sauce over the lentil mixture, and eat hot.

Moujaddra
Brown Lentils and Rice

Serves 4–6

1⅓ *cups whole brown lentils*
2 *onions, sliced into rings*
4 *tablespoons oil*
¼ *cup short-grain rice*

1 *tablespoon salt*
GARNISH:
crisply fried onion rings

Put the lentils in a saucepan, pour in about 1 quart of water, bring to a boil, then cover and simmer until the lentils are soft. Add more water if necessary. Cooking time will vary from 30–60 minutes depending on the age and size of the lentils. Drain.

Fry the onion rings in oil for 10–15 minutes, stirring occasionally, until golden-brown. Remove some rings for the garnish. Stir 2½ cups water into the pan and let the liquid boil and take up the color of the onions. Add this liquid to the cooked lentils.

Either press the lentil mixture through a strainer or purée in a food processor. Return the purée to the saucepan, add the rice and salt, then cook for an additional 15 minutes until the rice is tender and all the fluid absorbed. Serve hot or cold, garnished with fried onion rings.

Chick Peas with Yogurt and Bread

1⅛ *cups chick peas, soaked overnight*
2 *pita breads (page 31), toasted and torn into*
  pieces
1 *pot* labne *(page 30)*
2 *cloves garlic, crushed*

½ *teaspoon salt*
1 *teaspoon dried mint*
paprika
sprigs of parsley

Discard the soaking water, and cover the chick peas with fresh water. Bring to a boil and boil briskly for at least 10 minutes. Simmer for 1–1½ hours until tender, then drain and cool.

Place the pieces of pita bread in a serving dish, and moisten with some of the chick pea water. Mix together the *labne*, garlic, salt and mint, and stir in the chick peas, reserving some as a garnish. Spoon this over the bread. Garnish with the reserved chick peas, a sprinkling of paprika and parsley.

EGYPT
Ruzz
Egyptian Rice

1 scant cup long-grain rice
4 tablespoons butter

2½ cups water or *stock*
salt

Fry the rice in the butter for 2 minutes, stirring constantly. Add the water or stock, and bring to a boil. Cover and simmer for 20–35 minutes until all the water has been absorbed and the grains are fluffy. Season with salt, and toss well before serving.

IRAN
Chelo
Rice Cooked in Butter

Chelo is a very special Iranian way of serving rice. The rice is half cooked, then steamed in butter, and a golden crust is formed at the bottom of the pan.

1 lb. Basmati or *long-grain rice, soaked*
overnight

salt
1 stick (4 oz.) butter

Drain the rice, and boil in plenty of salted water for 8 minutes until still chewy. Drain, then rinse in warm water.

Melt half the butter in a large saucepan, adding 2 tablespoons water. Spoon the rice carefully into the pan, building it up to form a cone. Make three holes in the rice with a spoon handle to let out the steam. Melt the rest of the butter in a pan, then pour this over the rice. Heat until the steam rises, then cover with a tight-fitting lid, and cook over a low heat for 30 minutes until a crust forms at the bottom. Leave the pan to stand in cold water for 5 minutes to loosen the golden-brown crust.

Serve the white fluffy rice decorated with pieces of crust.

Chelo rice is often served with an egg yolk and *sumac*.

Sabzi Polo
Rice with Fresh Herbs
Serves 4–6

In Iran, *Sabzi* is the term given to a dish made from fresh herbs – usually a mixture of leeks, parsley, coriander and/or dill. Substitute dried herbs when fresh herbs are not available.

1 lb. Basmati or long-grain rice, soaked overnight
1 leek, minced
2 tablespoons minced fresh parsley or 1 tablespoon dried parsley flakes
2 tablespoons minced fresh dill or 1 tablespoon dried dill
2 tablespoons chopped cilantro
salt, freshly ground black pepper
6 tablespoons butter

Drain the rice, and cook in plenty of boiling water for 8 minutes until the rice is still chewy. Drain well, then place in a large bowl. Mix in the leek, parsley, dill, cilantro, salt and pepper.

Melt half the butter in a large saucepan, adding 2 tablespoons water. Carefully spoon in the rice mixture, building it up to form a cone. Make three holes in the rice with a spoon handle to let out the steam. Dot with the remaining butter. Heat until the rice begins to steam, then cover with a tight-fitting lid, and cook over gentle heat for 30 minutes until a crust forms at the bottom. Stand the saucepan in cold water for 5 minutes to loosen the golden-brown crust. Turn the rice out on to a serving dish, crust uppermost. Serve with fish dishes and yogurt.

Loubeigh Bil Zeit
Bean Salad
Serves 4–6

---

2 tablespoons oil
1 medium onion, sliced
2 cloves garlic

1 lb. green beans
16 oz. canned chopped tomatoes
salt, freshly ground black pepper

Heat the oil in a pan and fry the onion and garlic until soft. Stir in the beans, toss and fry for a few minutes until they soften. Add the tomatoes, salt and pepper. Bring to a boil, then cover and simmer for 20–30 minutes until the beans are tender. Leave to cool and serve cold as a salad or as part of the *mezze* table.

Arabian Bean Salad
Serves 6–8

A multi-colored bean dish served with an oil and lemon dressing.

1½ lb. different colored dried beans, soaked overnight (red kidney beans, black eyed peas, navy beans, fava beans, Egyptian brown beans, chick peas, green lentils)

DRESSING:
1 small onion, grated
1 dried red chili pepper, crumbled
⅔ cup olive oil
juice of 3 lemons
salt, freshly ground black pepper

Discard the soaking water, and cover the beans with fresh water. Bring to boil and boil briskly for at least 10 minutes. Simmer for 1½–2 hours until tender, then drain and rinse in cold water, and leave to cool.

Mix together all the ingredients for the dressing, and pour this over cooled beans. Toss the beans lightly in the dressing as some are softer than others and may break up.

A Selection of Bean Salads
*Bean Salad, Chick Pea, Tomato and Bulgur
Salad (page 76) and Arabian Bean Salad*

Chick Pea, Tomato and Bulgur Salad
Serves 2–4

---

²/₃ cup chick peas, soaked overnight
1 medium onion, finely chopped
2 tablespoons oil
8 oz. canned chopped tomatoes

²/₃ cup medium bulgur
1¼ cups water
salt, freshly ground black pepper

Discard the soaking water, and cover the chick peas with fresh water. Bring to a boil and boil briskly for at least 10 minutes. Simmer for 1–1½ hours until tender, then drain.

Fry the onion in the oil until soft. Stir in the tomatoes, and cook for 5 minutes until the sauce thickens. Add the bulgur, water, salt and pepper, and the cooked chick peas. Cover and cook for 20 minutes.

Avocado, Orange and Melon Salad
Serves 4–6

DRESSING:
2 tablespoons olive oil
1 tablespoon wine vinegar
½ teaspoon chili powder
½ teaspoon salt

freshly ground black pepper
1 scallion, minced
2 avocados skinned, pitted and sliced
2 oranges, peeled and thinly sliced
½ ripe honeydew melon, cut into chunks

Shake together all the dressing ingredients in a screw-top jar. Place the avocados, oranges and melon in a large bowl, and pour on the dressing. Toss and chill for 1 hour before serving.

ISRAEL
Date and Apple Salad
Serves 4–6

2 red apples, cored and sliced
juice of ½ lemon
⅔ cup mayonnaise
2 tablespoons plain yogurt

¼ lb. fresh dates, pitted and quartered
¼ cup chopped walnuts
½ head crisp lettuce, shredded

Toss the apples in the lemon juice. Mix together the mayonnaise and yogurt in a large bowl. Add the dates, apples and walnuts, and stir until coated with the mayonnaise. Serve on a bed of shredded lettuce.

IRAQ
Salatet Basel Wa Sumaq
Onion Salad with Sumac

2 onions, sliced into rings
1 teaspoon sumac *(see reference on page 9)*

pinch of salt

Toss the onion rings in the *sumac* and salt, and leave for 30 minutes to soften and absorb the flavor of the spice. Serve as a side dish, with kebabs.

SAUDI ARABIA
Saudi Salad

1 cucumber, diced
4 tomatoes, finely chopped
2 carrots, finely diced
bunch of radishes, finely chopped

4–6 scallions, minced
2 tablespoons fresh chopped parsley
salt
3 tablespoons wine vinegar

Mix the cucumber, tomatoes, carrots, radishes, scallions and parsley in a bowl. Before serving, sprinkle with salt and vinegar, and toss well.

Fattoush
Bread Salad

Serves 4–6

1 pita bread
1/2 head lettuce, shredded
1/2 red sweet pepper, cut into strips
1 bunch scallions, chopped
2–3 tomatoes, finely chopped
2 tablespoons fresh chopped parsley

1 tablespoon fresh chopped mint or 1 teaspoon
   dried mint
juice of 1–2 lemons
1/4 cup olive oil
salt, freshly ground black pepper
1/2 teaspoon ground cinnamon

Bake or broil the bread to dry it out. Break into small pieces, and set aside.
Place the remaining ingredients in a large salad bowl. Toss well, then chill.
Just before serving, toss in the pieces of bread.

IRAN
Borani Esfanaj
Spinach and Yogurt Salad

Serves 4–6

2 tablespoons oil
1 lb. fresh spinach, coarsely shredded
1 small onion, minced

2/3 cup strained yogurt or plain yogurt
1 clove garlic, crushed
salt, freshly ground black pepper

Heat the oil in a large saucepan and fry the onion for 2–3 minutes. Stir in the
spinach, toss well, then cover with a tight-fitting lid, and cook gently in its
own steam until soft. Add water if necessary. Cool, then mix in the yogurt,
garlic, salt and pepper.

Fattoush

Lentil Salad

1⅛ cups dried whole brown or *green lentils,*
  soaked overnight
1 clove garlic, crushed
1 teaspoon ground coriander
4 scallions, cut into fine rings

1 teaspoon salt
freshly ground black pepper
juice of 1–2 lemons
2 tablespoons olive oil
handful of fresh parsley, chopped

Discard the soaking water, put the lentils in a large saucepan, and cover with plenty of boiling water. Bring to a boil, then simmer for 30–50 minutes until tender, depending on the age and size of the lentils. Drain well. While still warm, stir in the garlic, coriander, scallions, salt, pepper, lemon juice, oil and parsley. Serve warm or cold.

DESSERTS & DRINKS

The abundance of fresh fruit in the Middle East is often served as dessert. Included in the great variety are melons, many types of citrus fruit, mangoes, figs, dates, pomegranates and apricots.

As a contrast, Middle Eastern pastries and cakes are extraordinarily sweet, usually made from butter, flour, different nuts, such as pistachios, walnuts or almonds, soaked in a honey or sugar-rich syrup.

Milk puddings, made from rice or ground rice, are also very popular and are served with syrup or honey and a scattering of nuts.

Since, for religious reasons, the drinking of alcohol is forbidden in many Middle Eastern countries, there are many deliciously refreshing drinks made from fruits, orange blossoms or rosewater. Sherbert originated in Iran, from which "sorbet" is thought to have evolved. Sherberts are made from fruit syrups, such as oranges or pomegranates, and served with cold water over plenty of crushed ice.

In Middle Eastern countries, thick Turkish coffee is drunk throughout the day, sometimes flavored with crushed cardamoms. In Iraq and Iran, however, tea is the most popular drink.

Halva is the name given to Arabic sweet dishes, particularly those which are like thick pastes. Halva is usually served with coffee or tea and may be eaten with a spoon or cut into pieces.

Without a doubt, a sweet tooth cannot fail to be satisfied by Middle Eastern cookery!

IRAN
Halva

In Iran, this halva is served after the wedding feast, and each guest is given a portion to take home. Halva needs careful cooking as the mixture burns easily.

1 teaspoon powdered saffron
1 teaspoon sugar
⅔ cup boiling water
1 cup sugar
1 scant cup oil

4 cups all-purpose flour
2 tablespoons rose water
DECORATION:
chopped pistachios or slivered almonds

Mix together the saffron and 1 teaspoon sugar. Boil the saffron, water and sugar in a saucepan until the sugar has dissolved. Leave to cool.

Heat the oil in a saucepan, then stir in the flour. Beat and stir over the heat until the flour starts to change to a golden-brown color and becomes sandy in texture. This may take 25–35 minutes. Take care not to burn the mixture. Add the rose water and 4 tablespoons of the saffron liquid. Cook for an additional 10–15 minutes until the mixture thickens once more.

Spread the mixture on a plate, and decorate with chopped nuts. Cool until firm. Guests may take thin slices to be eaten with a fork or spoon.

IRAQ
Date Halva

1⅓ cups pitted dates, finely chopped
½ cup chopped walnuts
½ cup chopped almonds

¼ teaspoon ground cinnamon
¼ teaspoon ground allspice
confectioner's sugar for dusting

Mix the dates, nuts and spices in a bowl, using your hands to work the ingredients together.

Dust a work surface with confectioner's sugar, and roll out the halva to about ¾-inch thickness. Cut into squares, and sprinkle with confectioner's sugar.

Date Halva

Stuffed Fresh Dates

½ lb. fresh dates
STUFFING:
⅓ cup walnuts

½ teaspoon allspice
a little lemon juice

Remove the date pits by cutting lengthwise with a knife.

To make the stuffing, grind the walnuts to a smooth paste, stir in the allspice, then add lemon juice, if necessary, to make the mixture stick together.

Roll the stuffing into small sausage shapes, and use to stuff into the dates.

Muhallabia
Rice Pudding

Serves 4–6

Muhallabia is eaten throughout the Middle East and is served chilled and decorated with sugar syrup and chopped nuts.

½ cup rice flour
3 tablespoons cornstarch
5 cups milk
⅓ cup sugar
3 tablespoons orange blossom water or rose water

1 cup ground almonds (optional)
DECORATION:
Atter *(page 92)*
chopped pistachios or almonds

Mix together the rice flour and cornstarch, and blend to a smooth paste with some of the milk. Boil the rest of the milk in a large pan, then stir in the blended mixture. Heat, stirring constantly until the mixture thickens and coats the back of a spoon. Add the sugar and orange blossom or rose water, and bring to a boil. Stir in the ground almonds, if used. Pour into serving dishes and chill. Serve with a little *Atter* poured over the top and a sprinkling of nuts.

EGYPT
Batata Pie
Sweet Potato Pudding

Serves 4–6

In Egypt, baked sweet potatoes are sold by street vendors during winter months. This recipe uses them for a pudding.

1½ lb. sweet potatoes, cleaned, peeled and
chopped
4 tablespoons butter
2 tablespoons honey
1 teaspoon grated nutmeg

pinch of ground ginger
⅔ cup milk
2 eggs, beaten
⅓ cup chopped dates (optional)

Boil the sweet potatoes in water for 20 minutes until soft. Drain, then mash them with butter. Beat in the honey, nutmeg and ginger. Mix together the milk and eggs, and stir into the mixture. Pour into a greased ovenproof dish, and sprinkle with the chopped dates, if used. Bake in a moderate oven (350°F) for about 45 minutes until the pudding is firm.

Serve hot with cream.

IRAN
Shir Brenj
Persian Rice Pudding

½ cup long-grain rice
2 cups water
2½ cups milk
1 tablespoon rose water

pinch of salt
¼ cup granulated sugar
ground cinnamon

Cook the rice uncovered, in the water for 20–25 minutes until the water is absorbed. Add the milk, rose water, salt and sugar, bring to a boil and simmer for 25 minutes. Pour into a serving dish, sprinkle with cinnamon, and leave to cool.

Serve with honey, if desired.

Khoshaf
Dried Fruit Salad

During Ramadan, Muslims often end their fast with a meal of beans, meat balls, kebabs and this dried fruit salad.

⅔ cup dried apricots
⅔ cup prunes
⅔ cup dried figs
6 tablespoons seedless raisins

2 tablespoons orange blossom water or rose water
6 tablespoons pine nuts or slivered almonds

Soak the dried fruit overnight, then drain and place in a saucepan. Cover with boiling water, and simmer for 20–30 minutes until the fruit is tender. Stir in the orange blossom or rose water, and serve hot or cold, sprinkled with nuts.

Q'Aqib Agwa
Date and Pastry Rolls

1 stick (4 oz.) unsalted butter
2 cups all-purpose flour
2 tablespoons water
confectioner's sugar, sifted

FILLING:
⅔ cup dates, pitted
2 tablespoons butter
½ teaspoon ground cinnamon
1 teaspoon rose water

Melt the butter and work it into the flour in a large bowl. Stir in the water, then knead with your hands to form a smooth dough. Cover with plastic wrap, then leave to cool and relax for 30 minutes.

To make the filling, grind or pound the dates to a smooth paste. Place them in a small pan with the butter, cinnamon and rose water, and heat gently, stirring until a smooth paste has formed. Spread on a plate to cool.

Divide the dough into about 20 pieces, then form into small balls. Flour the work surface and roll each ball out into a 3-inch circle. Place some of the date mixture in a strip down one end, and roll up like a cigar. Place on a greased baking sheet with the seam underneath. Bake in a moderately hot oven (375°F) for 15–20 minutes until a light golden color. Leave to cool, then sprinkle with confectioner's sugar.

Khoshaf

ISRAEL
Sharon Fruit, Pomegranate and Kumquat Salad
Serves 4–6

The Israeli sharon fruit has a sweet orange-colored flesh, with no pips, and may be eaten firm or soft. It gets its name from the Plains of Sharon in Israel.

6 sharon fruit
2 pomegranates
2 tablespoons pomegranate juice (page 10) or
  2 tablespoons lemon juice

8–10 kumquats, sliced
a little sugar to taste

Slice the top off each sharon fruit, and cut into sections. Remove the seeds from one pomegranate by cutting the fruit in half, then pressing it gently with the fingers while knocking the hard skin with a knife handle.

Squeeze the juice from the other pomegranate; either use a lemon squeezer or, the local way, squeeze the fruit to loosen the seeds, then make a hole in the skin and squeeze out the juice. Mix this juice with the ready-made pomegranate juice or lemon juice, then add a little water and sugar if required.

Place all the ingredients in a large glass dish, and chill before serving.

EGYPT
Mehallabiyet Bortoqan
Orange Pudding

3 cups fresh orange juice
½ cup rice flour or ¼ cup cornstarch

1 orange
2 oz. granulated sugar

Heat the orange juice and ground rice, stirring until the mixture thickens. Grate the rind from the orange and add to the mixture with the sugar. Bring to a boil and pour into serving dishes. Trim any pith from the oranges, cut them into sections, and decorate the dishes with them. Serve chilled.

Kunafeh
Shredded Buttery Pastry with Creamy Filling
Serves 6–8

The ready-made *kunafeh* pastry means that the dish is very quick to prepare, yet looks like a work of great skill!

FILLING:
¼ cup rice flour
2 tablespoons sugar
1¼ cups milk
few drops vanilla extract

1¼ cups Atter (page 92)
PASTRY:
8 oz. ready-made kunafeh pastry
1 stick (4 oz.) unsalted butter

Prepare the filling first. Blend the rice flour and sugar to a smooth paste with a little of the milk. Boil the rest of the milk, pour into the rice flour mixture, stir and return to the saucepan. Heat, stirring constantly, until the sauce thickens. Add the vanilla extract.

Prepare the pastry. Place the *kunafeh* in a large bowl, and gently pull the strands apart. Melt the butter, and pour it over the pastry. Toss with a fork until all the strands are coated.

Grease an 8 inch-square baking pan. Spread on half the pastry, then pour on the filling. Cover with the remaining pastry, and press down with the hands. Cook for 40–45 minutes in a moderately hot oven (375°F) until light golden-brown. Pour the cold syrup evenly over the hot pastry, then cut into rectangles or squares. Serve hot or cold.

Baklava
Nut Filled Pastries

²⁄₃ *cup* Atter *(page 92)*
²⁄₃ *cup butter*
8 oz. phyllo *pastry*
FILLING:
1¼ cups finely chopped almonds

1¼ cups finely chopped walnuts
1 teaspoon ground cinnamon
1 teaspoon ground allspice
¼ cup granulated sugar
2 tablespoons rose water

Prepare the *Atter*, and set aside to cool.

Mix together all the ingredients for the filling.

Melt the butter. Grease a 12 × 8 × 2 inch baking pan.

Open out the sheets of *phyllo* pastry, and keep the pastry covered with a dish towel to prevent drying out. Lay a sheet of *phyllo* pastry in the baking pan, and brush with some of the butter. Cover with 9 more sheets of pastry, buttering each layer. Spread on the nut filling, then cover with 10 more sheets of pastry, again buttering each layer. Butter the top especially well to prevent the pastry from springing up.

With a sharp knife, score diagonal lines through to the nut filling, then cross them, forming diamond shapes. Bake in a moderately hot oven (375°F) for 20–25 minutes until the baklava is crisp and golden. Allow the baklava to cool slightly before pouring over about ²⁄₃ cup *Atter*. Cut into diamond shapes. Serve cold accompanied by syrup or cream.

Baklava and *Kunafeh (page 89)*

Atter
Blossom Syrup

This syrup may be stored in the refrigerator for several months. It can be poured over pastries such as *Baklava* (page 90) or used for rice puddings like *Muhallabia* (page 84).

2 cups granulated sugar
2 cups water
juice of ½ lemon

3 tablespoons rose water or *orange blossom water*

Heat the sugar, water and lemon juice in a saucepan for 15–20 minutes, stirring occasionally until the syrup begins to thicken. Skim the surface, then stir in the rose water or orange blossom water, and leave to cool.

Note: Use the syrup cold over warm pastries, but warm up the syrup if the pastry is cold, otherwise it will not spread evenly.

Arabic Coffee
Serves 2

True Arabic coffee is served black, with a little sugar and sometimes spices. Traditionally, the coffee is made in a small pot with a narrow neck and long handle.

4 teaspoons dark-roasted, finely ground coffee

2 demitasse cups of water
2 teaspoons sugar

Boil the water, then stir in the coffee and sugar, using a long handled spoon. Allow the coffee to boil until it foams. Remove from the heat and leave the coffee to settle, then serve.

Raisin Tea

Serves 2

⅔ cup seedless raisins
1¼ cups water

ground cinnamon

Soak the raisins overnight in the water, then bring to a boil. Simmer for 30 minutes until soft, then strain or pulverize the mixture in an electric blender together with a pinch of ground cinnamon. Chill before serving.

Lemonada
Fresh Lemon Drink

Serves 2–4

---

juice of 3 lemons
2–3 tablespoons sugar

2 tablespoons orange blossom or rose water
ice cubes

Mix together the lemon juice, sugar and blossom water, and stir until the sugar dissolves. Dilute to taste with ice-cold water and serve with ice cubes. Sugar quantities can be adjusted to taste.

Aseer Romman
Pomegranate Drink

---

2 large pomegranates
1¼ cups ice water
1 teaspoon rose water

sugar to taste
juice of ½ lemon

Remove the seeds from the pomegranate, (see page 88) and blend all the ingredients in a food processor or rub through a strainer.

MENUS

Entertaining Friends for Dinner

Avocado Soup (page 17)

•

Chicken Stuffed with Rice, Almonds and Golden Raisins
(page 62)

•

Rice with Fresh Herbs (page 73)

•

Saudi Salad (page 77)

•

Sharon Fruit, Pomegranate and Kumquat Salad (page 88)

•

Date Halva (page 82)